Christmas Together

25 Hymns, Prayers, Recipes, and Activities to Celebrate Christmas With Our Families

TONNA O'DELL

WestBow Press books may be ordered through booksellers or by contacting:

WestBow Press
A Division of Thomas Nelson & Zondervan
1663 Liberty Drive
Bloomington, IN 47403
www.westbowpress.com
1 (866) 928-1240

ISBN: 978-1-9736-2258-1 (sc)
ISBN: 978-1-9736-2259-8 (e)

Library of Congress Control Number: 2018903191

Print information available on the last page.

WestBow Press rev. date: 04/17/2018

WESTBOW
PRESS®
A DIVISION OF THOMAS NELSON
& ZONDERVAN

For Lydia and Phoebe

I hope that the scriptures, hymns, prayers, recipes, activities, and mission ideas in this book will influence you and stick with you throughout your life. May you share them with your family one day and make memories of your own as you reflect on our time spent *together.*

Mom and Dad

Words cannot express how grateful I am for the love and guidance you have given me all my life. You made sure to fill our home with fun and laughter and those memories will always be remembered with joy in my heart. Most of all, I am thankful for the example of your faith in the Lord. Your commitment to God and the church has taught me what being a true disciple means.

In Loving Memory of Aunt Dar, Grandpa Roy, and Grandma Rachel

Thank you for your legacy of love and your example of what it means to follow Christ. You are now singing with Jesus and I eagerly anticipate the day that I can join you around the throne in praises to our King.

Eric

Thank you for believing in this book and making it possible. I love you and am so blessed to journey through life with you.

Merry CHRISTMAS

INTRODUCTION

Twelve years ago, my husband and I became parents for the first time to a beautiful baby girl. Then, less than three years later, we were blessed with another little girl who captured all of our hearts immediately. Our precious daughters have taught us many lessons in the short years that God has entrusted them to us. But in the past few years we have come to understand even deeper something that we already knew.

Life gets really hectic with jobs, schoolwork and activities. It's easy to get caught up in the competition with our kids to be the "best" at school, sports, and other activities. While it's always important to teach our kids to try their best and set their goals high, our greatest concern is the health of their precious souls. We know that God has gifted each of them with unique personalities and talents and it is our responsibility to help them use those talents for God's glory.

We are learning as a family that our faith grows deepest when we slow down. This approach may seem odd by today's standard of "doing life." But we are discovering that this slower pace is just how our family rolls, so to speak. We know that we cannot slow down how fast our kids are growing up, but we can slow down and enjoy every moment we are blessed with them. When we sing *together*, play *together*, cook *together*, laugh *together*, and just simply be *together*, we are strengthening a bond that God intended to be strong…the bond of family. Slowing down is when we make memories together and are able to reflect on our faith.

Some of my greatest memories growing up are from Christmastime as we celebrated the season *together*. I can remember how excited my sister and I would get when Dad would come home from his construction job and begin stringing lights on the tree. We only had one family tree that we all decorated *together*. Singing as a family was also something that my family did traditionally at Christmas. My Grandpa would grab his guitar, my sister would play the piano and generations would all gather around to sing *together*. One of the tastiest memories is making Christmas candy and treats with my

Grandma. It was normal for her kitchen to smell like sugar and spice all season long from pies, cookies, and cakes to hard rock candy and fudge.

The last several years have taught us that our main goal as parents is to help lay a firm foundation of Christ in our children's lives so that they will be able to withstand any storm that might assail against them in life. Being a Christian means we are called to make disciples and that discipleship should begin in our homes with our own children. We must teach and model to them that with Christ as our foundation, the world will grow strangely dim. Living for eternity is what matters most in life, and keeping that perspective is essential in our desire to become more like Jesus. What a gift it is to put all the busyness of life aside and just rest in Jesus *together* as a family.

So that brings us to the purpose of this book – *Christmas Together*. Celebrating Jesus' birth is something that we should be excited about with our families. When I realized more and more that Jesus was pushed aside by the hectic schedule of the holiday season, I asked God to show me how to make Christmas more meaningful for my family and more about Jesus. I wanted us to focus on the real reason for the season and at the same time find Jesus in the "fun" family traditions. God was telling me that Jesus could be found in all the singing, baking, crafts, decorating, and traditions that we already do at Christmastime. I didn't have to plan completely special moments but just simply join Jesus in the celebration.

In this book, you will be encouraged each day from December 1st to December 25th to:

* Read a Scripture Verse *Together*
* Sing *Together*
* Pray *Together*
* Cook *Together*
* Have Fun *Together*

You will also find four *On Mission Together* activities to do as a family. These are designed to help direct our faith in Christ to sharing Him with others who might not know about Jesus.

It's my desire that families will celebrate Christmas knowing that Jesus can be found in the middle of their traditions. Look for teachable moments and ask your kids questions about the Christmas story. We know that Christ was born to save and this is the most important truth of the Christmas season. Imagine all the conversations that our families will have this Christmas. But most of all, may we seek Him, find Him, and be filled with abundant joy. May our families grow deeper in our faith and further be compelled to share the Gospel with the world.

ON MISSION

TOGETHER

"For, everyone who calls on the name of the Lord will be saved. How, then, can they call on the one they have not believed in? And how can they believe in the one of whom they have not heard? And how can they hear without someone preaching to them?"
Romans 10:13-14

8 Day Neighbor Nativity Mystery

Pick a neighbor to whom your family will deliver a piece of a nativity set each day for 8 days on their doorstep. The gift will not say who it's from, so the neighbor will open their front door each day from December 1-8 and find a small gift waiting for them and wonder who it's from! What fun! On day 8, deliver baby Jesus (and reveal who the gift giver is to the neighbor).

Share the gospel and have Christmas fun at the same time!

Write the following on gift tags to correspond to each day's nativity gift.

Day 1:   Long ago, God promised that a little town named Bethlehem would be where Jesus, the Savior of the world, would be born. There was a stable in

Bethlehem with a manger. The manger was filled with hay for the animals to eat. One of the animals there was a **COW**.

Day 2:   There was also a **DONKEY** in that stable.

Day 3:   Then one day to the animal's surprise, a young woman came to the stable to stay for the night. Cesar Augustus had sent out a decree that all the citizens of the Roman world should be taxed and counted in their hometowns. The tiny town of Bethlehem was filled with people, so all the inns were full and there was no room. The woman's name was **MARY** and she was going to have a baby and needed somewhere to rest.

Day 4:   Traveling with her was a man named **JOSEPH**, to whom she was engaged to be married. An angel of God came to him in a dream before they traveled and told him, "This baby is from God. His name shall be called Jesus, for he will save his people from their sins." The prophets had foretold about the birth of this baby long ago.

Day 5:   **SHEPHERDS** were in the fields surrounding Bethlehem.

Day 6:   They were tending their **SHEEP**.

Day 7:   In the fields where the shepherds were tending their flocks, an **ANGEL OF THE LORD** appeared. The shepherds were greatly afraid but the angel said, "Fear not. I bring you good news of great joy that will be for all the people. For unto you is born this day in the city of David a Savior, who is Christ the Lord. You will find a baby wrapped in swaddling clothes and lying in a manger." And then all of the sudden there was a great host of angels saying, "Glory to God in the highest!"

Day 8:   The shepherds went to find Mary and Joseph in the stable. And there they found the **BABY JESUS** lying in a manger.

DECEMBER 1

"In the sixth month, God sent the angel Gabriel to Nazareth, a town in Galilee, to a virgin pledged to be married to a man named Joseph, a descendent of David. The virgin's name was Mary."
Luke 1:26-27

Sing Together

Come Thou Long Expected Jesus

So often, we see our sin and weakness and think that God could never use us. We ask, "Why would God ever ask someone like me to do something so big?" But that's just the way God works. He is in the business of using what we see as our weaknesses and working through us for His glory. In Luke chapter 1, God chooses Mary to be the mother of Jesus. She was not married and very young. Mary was an unlikely choice by man's standards, but God had a plan!

Pray Together

Dear God, thank You for this glorious season in which we celebrate Your birth. May we approach this time of year with joy in our hearts and find reasons every day to glorify You.

Cook Together

Lydia and Phoebe's Snicker Doodle Cookies

. . . .

2 ¾ cup all purpose-flour   ¼ tsp. salt

1 ¾ cups sugar   1 ½ tsp. vanilla extract

1 tsp. baking powder   1 cup (2 sticks) unsalted butter (melted)

2 large eggs   1 tsp. ground cinnamon

Preheat the oven to 350 degrees. Line a cookie sheet with parchment paper. In a bowl, whisk together the flour, baking powder, and salt. In another bowl, using an electric mixer, beat the butter and 1 ½ cups of sugar on medium speed until well blended, about 1 minute. Add the eggs and vanilla and beat on low speed until combined. Turn off the mixer and scrape down the bowl with a rubber spatula. Add the flour mixture and mix just until blended.

In a small bowl, stir together the remaining ¼ cup sugar and the cinnamon. Scoop up rounded tablespoons of dough and roll into a ball. Drop the ball into the sugar/cinnamon mixture and roll it to coat it completely. Place the balls on the cookie sheet about 3 inches apart. Bake the cookies for 10 to 12 minutes. Let cool for 5 minutes and use a metal spatula to move them.

Fun Together

Send out Christmas cards to your family, friends, and neighbors.

Let each family member have a job such as stuffing the card in the envelope, licking the envelope, addressing the card, or sticking on the stamp. Take time to share memories about each person you are addressing a card to and say a special prayer for them.

DECEMBER 2

"But the angel said to her, "Do not be afraid, Mary, you have found favor with God."
Luke 1:30

Sing Together

Oh, Come, Oh, Come Emmanuel

. . . .

Mary was not rich or royalty, but she was exactly the girl that God wanted to be Jesus' mother. It stands to reason that she was scared and did not fully understand what the angel was telling her. But Mary was faithful and was a part of God's plan. Just like Mary, there will be times when God calls us and we don't feel adequate. But He desires our obedience and like Mary, we can give Jesus to the world.

Pray Together

Jesus, we are so grateful that You loved us so much that You left heaven and came to Earth as a baby. You did this to rescue us from our sin and eternal death. Thank You for Your gift of love.

Cook Together

Grandma Rachel's Froot Loop Candy

. . . .

Froot Loop Cereal   White Chocolate Almond Bark

Miniature Marshmallows

Melt the almond bark in 30 second intervals stirring in between each interval. Mix in Froot Loops and marshmallows liberally. Use a spoon to scoop out on parchment paper. Let cool and they will harden.

Fun Together

Paint Christmas ornaments.

*clear plastic ornament balls

*2 or more colors of paint in original squeeze bottles

Place a drop cloth onto the table to protect it from paint spills. Squeeze a bit of paint into the open ornament ball. Rotate the ornament a bit and add a squeeze of different color. Roll the ornament in your hands, shake it, or do whatever you'd like to move the paint around to get a marbled affect. Add as much paint as necessary until the entire inside is covered in paint. Put the ornaments in an empty egg carton upside down to let the extra paint drip out. Let them dry for one day. Put the top of the ornament back on and add string once they are dry.

DECEMBER 3

"You will be with child and give birth to a son, and
you are to give him the name Jesus."
Luke 1:31

Sing Together

What Child is This?

....

What can we learn from Mary? We can ask ourselves what our weaknesses are and how God can use us to accomplish His purposes. Sometimes we just need to change our perspective or attitude so Jesus can be glorified in our lives. God often times works through us in our most difficult circumstances because this is when we are most dependent upon Him. We need to be willing to trust God during our trials and give Him all the glory.

Pray Together

God, we join with all of heaven and sing Your praise. You are great and greatly to be praised. We find our joy in You and You alone!

Cook Together

Coconut Bon Bon's

....

1 can sweetened condensed milk

2 or 4 cups chopped nuts (optional)

1 package (12 oz.) coconut

2 sticks butter melted

2 boxes powdered sugar

Mix all the ingredients in a large bowl and put in the refrigerator for 2 hours. After they have chilled, roll in small balls and dip in melted chocolate almond bark. Put on parchment paper to harden.

Fun Together

Make a Christmas wreath.

Trace both of your child's hands on green construction paper. Cut out enough hands to glue together to make a wreath. After the glue dries, tie a red ribbon around the top to hang it on their bedroom door. Encourage them to praise the Lord for the good things He has done every time they look at the wreath.

"So I will bless you as long as I live; I will lift up my hands in your name."
Psalm 64:4

DECEMBER 4

"He will be great and will be called the Son of the Most High. The Lord God will give him the throne of his father David."
Luke 1:32

Sing Together

O Come All Ye Faithful

....

Naturally, Mary wondered what the angel was saying and what was going to happen. But she questioned the angel from a place of faith not a place of doubt. She trusted and believed, but was curious about the circumstances that she would face. Mary is a true example of faith in the midst of the unknown. We should remember that it is okay to ask God questions but to always seek His will through His Holy Word. As we wait on Him, our faith will grow deeper.

Pray Together

Father, we adore You. We lift up Your name today and ask that You help us to be faithful servants for you.

Cook Together

Spice Tea

....

2 quarts apple juice

1 ½ cup cranberry juice

1 cup brown sugar

4 cinnamon sticks

Simmer together and enjoy!

Fun Together

Make graham cracker ginger bread houses.

Using graham crackers, white icing, and candy, have a family gingerbread house contest. Set a time limit and see who can build the most unique house that stands freely.

DECEMBER 5

"I am the Lord's servant," Mary answered. "May it be to
me as you have said." Then the angel left her.
Luke 1:38

Sing Together

Angels From the Realms of Glory

....

When we see in verse 38 how Mary responded, it is a great testimony of her submission
to God. What an amazing example of Mary's character and trust in her Lord. She was
young, but she was a girl of deep faith and obedience. May we always submit to God
and seek His will despite our age and experience in this life. Trusting Him is always in our
best interest because we are becoming more like Jesus.

Pray Together

Lord God, we know that we are sinners and are need of your grace. We thank You that
You so freely gave Your Son so that we may live.

Cook Together

Grandma's Home-made chocolate fudge

....

½ pound butter (8 oz. or 1 cup)   4 cups sugar

1 large can evaporated milk   1/8 tsp. salt

Cook in thick pan and stir constantly until it comes to soft ball stage in water.

Have ready:

1 large marshmallow cream   2 packages chocolate chips

Pour hot mixture over the marshmallow cream and 2 packages of chocolate chips. Stir in until chips melt and all is mixed. Pour into 2 greased pans. Cool at room temperature. Cut into squares.

Fun Together

Make gift tags.

Use a variety of scrapbook paper with varying patterns. Have fun creating home-made and unique gift tags!

DECEMBER 6

"In those days Caesar Augustus issued a decree that a census should be taken of the entire Roman world."

Luke 2:1

Sing Together

THE BIRTHDAY OF A KING

When it is hard to be obedient to God's will and plan, it is easy to be tempted to give up and take the easier road. Some days are easier to obey than others and sometimes our own plans seem to make more sense than Gods. In Luke chapter 2, Mary and Joseph were called to Bethlehem to pay their taxes during the census of the Roman Empire. This was a long journey. Talk about having faith and trust!

Pray Together

Jesus, we are very happy to be celebrating Your birthday. We know that You became flesh to redeem us from our sins and we thank You for being mindful of us.

Cook Together

Mom's Hard Rock Candy

....

*3 ¾ cups sugar   *1 cup water

*1 ¼ cup white syrup   *1 teaspoon red food coloring

Stir with wooden spoon over medium heat and bring to a boil. Cover and cook for 3 minutes. Then uncover and cook at least ½ hour until candy thermometer reaches 300 degrees. (about 25 minutes)

Turn off heat. Add 1 ¼ teaspoon cinnamon oil. (DO NOT BREATHE VAPOR DIRECTLY)

Line cookie sheet with aluminum foil and pour candy mixture onto it. Dust with powdered sugar.

Fun Together

Watch a Christmas movie.

Let the kids pick the movie and pop some popcorn.
Snuggle up with warm blankets too!

DECEMBER 7

"And everyone went to his own town to register."
Luke 2:3

Sing Together

O Little Town of Bethlehem

••

Going to Bethlehem at this point in Mary's pregnancy was not going to be easy nor did it seem wise to make the rough journey. Traveling would be very uncomfortable for her, but she was faithful. Joseph and Mary left their home and walked hundreds of miles for the census and all the way they trusted in God. Having this kind of trust can be so very difficult, but also so rewarding. May we learn more every day about how important it is to trust God in all things.

Pray Together

Dear God, we humbly ask You to abide in our hearts. For we know You are with us, Emmanuel. Cleanse us from all our sin and purify our hearts.

Cook Together

Granny's Pecan Pie

....

Mix with a mixer

*3 eggs   *1/3 cup melted butter

*2/3 cup sugar   *Dash of salt

*1 cup corn syrup

Pour mixture into unbaked pie shell. Place 1 cup pecan halves on top and bake at 350 degrees for 50 minutes.

Fun Together

Have an indoor snowball fight.

Find an open space but yet a place with furniture that you can possibly hide behind also. Use white loofah sponges to look like snowballs. Team up and have a snowball fight.

ON MISSION

TOGETHER

"Declare His glory among the nations, His marvelous deeds among all peoples."
Psalm 96:3

Stocking Surprise

My family is by no means rich monetarily, but we are living a "comfortable" life by definition. Sometimes there is a feeling of guilt attached to the knowledge of what we've been blessed with when so many others around us are hurting and in need. We see the need locally and internationally. We often talk with our children about how God calls us to give since we have been given much. We know that there is more we can do as a family to meet the physical needs of children in our area.

So the idea of a Stocking Surprise was born. This is a stocking that we hang up somewhere prominent in our house. Over the Christmas season we will add small gifts to the stocking. Before Christmas we will deliver the stocking to the Children's Home in our area and the items can be distributed among the children there.

Our gifts can be for boys or girls since the gifts will be divided among the children in the home. This is a way to help us remember to stay mindful of others during the season and to love because He first loved us. We are commanded to love our neighbor and this is just one small way we can do that as a family.

Some suggested items to put in the stocking:

*chap stick	*body spray
*deodorant	*playing cards
*tooth paste	*pens
*tooth brush	*pencils
*hair accessories	*journal
*hair brush/comb	*candy

Before you deliver your stocking, take time to write a letter letting the children at the home know about your family. Wish them a very Merry Christmas, but most importantly, share that Christ was born to save. Remind them that they have not been forgotten, for Christ knows them each by name and knows every hair on their head. May this small stocking of gifts help them feel loved by your family but mostly by the Savior.

DECEMBER 8

"So Joseph also went up from the town of Nazareth in Galilee to Judea, to Bethlehem the town of David, because he belonged to the house and line of David. He went there to register with Mary, who was pledged to be married to him and was expecting a child."
Luke 2:4-5

Sing Together

Jesus is Lord of All

This long and treacherous journey to Bethlehem was not in Joseph and Mary's plan. But it was part of God's plan according to prophesy. They trusted God to provide for them and protect them.

At times in life, we too will be tempted to neglect or feel angry about God's plan, but we can always trust that He wants what is best for us. And what is always best for us is to become more like Jesus. We are refined in the trials and grow in grace when we face insurmountable odds. God's plan is always perfect!

Pray Together

Thank You Jesus for coming down from heaven. You are Lord of all and over all things. We give our lives to you. Guide and direct our paths.

Cook Together

Grandma Clinton's Coconut Cookies

1 cup soft butter

1 cup granulated sugar

½ cup firmly packed brown sugar

2 cups unsifted flour

2 eggs

2 tsp. vanilla

1 tsp. baking soda

1 tsp. salt

7 oz. coconut

Bake at 325 degrees for about 10 minutes. Take them out the oven when they actually look like they are not done and they will finish cooking on the stove.

Fun Together

Put together a Christmas puzzle.

Pick out a puzzle that tells part of the Christmas story. A nativity puzzle, for example, would be great to do. This will be an activity that will take plenty of days or nights to work on. As you work on the puzzle together, talk about the Christmas story and why Christ came to save us.

DECEMBER 9

"While they were there, the time came for the baby to be born,"
Luke 2:6

Sing Together

Away in a Manger

So what do we do when obedience to God is not easy? When we are tempted to give up on something that we know God has called us to, we need to pray and ask for strength. Just like Mary, we are going to face times when Jesus has called us to do something that seems impossible. But He sends His grace to us and through Him, we can conquer our fears.

Pray Together

Help us to think about how humble a place You were born Lord. You became completely human to identify with us, yet You were fully God to redeem us. You know us and understand us better than anyone else ever could.

Cook Together

Happy Birthday Jesus Cupcakes

....

Bake any flavor of cake into cupcakes. You can even use holiday cupcake liners to make them look more festive. When cool, add the butter cream icing.

Butter Cream Icing

1 stick butter (softened)

½ cup Crisco

1 tsp. Vanilla

4 cups powdered sugar (one at a time)

3 tbs. milk

Once you have put the icing on the cupcakes, you may add colorful sprinkles!

Fun Together

Draw a Christmas picture of the manger where Jesus was born.

Using black construction paper and colored chalk, draw a picture of the stable where Jesus was born. Add in as many details to the picture as you can. When the pictures are finished, tell about your picture and what you drew. Repeat the sounding joy!!

DECEMBER 10

"and she gave birth to her firstborn, a son. She wrapped him in cloths and placed him in a manger, because there was no room for them in the inn."
Luke 2:7

Sing Together

Infant Holy, Infant Lowly

Mary's faith became her sight. In a simple barn, away from the city, the Savior of the world was born. Quietly He came, but the world would never be the same. That night in Bethlehem, Mary and Joseph beheld the immeasurable love of God!

Pray Together

Help us to think about how humble a place You were born Lord. You became completely human to identify with us, yet You were fully God to redeem us. You know us and understand us better than anyone else ever could.

Cook Together

Butterscotch Haystacks

....

*1 2/3 cups (11 –oz. pkg.)
Butterscotch Flavored morsels

1 can (8.5 oz.) or 2 cans (5 oz.
each) chow mein noodles

¾ cup creamy peanut butter

3 ½ cups miniature marshmallows

Line trays with wax paper

Microwave morsels in large, uncovered, microwave safe bowl for 1 minute.

Stir, and if necessary, microwave for an additional 10 to 15 seconds, stirring just until morsels are melted. Stir in peanut butter until blended well. Add chow mein noodles and marshmallows. Stir until mixed well. Spoon out onto wax paper and refrigerate until ready to serve.

Fun Together

Make swaddling clothes.

Get some scrap material and cut it into a wide strip. With a doll, practice swaddling the baby. As you do this, emphasize the fact that Jesus was human in every way and took on flesh. He felt all the same fears that we have felt and can identify with our needs as humans. He was God with us, God made man. Practice to see who can wrap the baby the fastest, but all the while discussing just how amazing it is that Jesus became a man to save us from our sins.

DECEMBER 11

"And there were shepherds living out in the fields nearby,
keeping watch over their flocks at night."
Luke 2:8

Sing Together

While Shepherds Watched Their Flocks

....

While Jesus was lying in the manger, as Mary and Joseph considered all that God had done, there were shepherds in the fields outside the city. They were some of the meekest, most humble members of society. While all of Bethlehem lay sleeping, the shepherds were keeping watch. God sometimes chooses to reveal Himself to the most unlikely group. Just like the shepherds, we must be ready to hear God and follow where He leads.

Pray Together

Glory to You God for all You have done! You have spoken peace in our hearts and told us not to fear. Help us to rest in the peace that only You can bring.

Cook Together

Oreo Balls

1 package Oreos

1 package cream cheese

Chocolate or White
Chocolate Almond Bark

Crush all the Oreos in a food processor. Soften the cream cheese and mix together with the crushed Oreos. Form spoon size balls with the mixture. Put them on a pan lined with parchment paper and chill them in the refrigerator for a few hours. Melt the almond bark and dip each ball into it. Once again place chocolate covered balls on parchment paper to let the chocolate harden.

Fun Together

Make hot chocolate with whipped cream and other fixings.

Heat water or milk and add pre-packaged hot chocolate mix. Let each family member add their own whip cream, marshmallows or peppermint sticks. Sprinkles on top of whip cream always make it more fun!

DECEMBER 12

"An angel of the Lord appeared to them, and the glory of the
Lord shone around them, and they were afraid."
Luke 2:9

Sing Together

Hark the Herald Angels Sing

....

The announcement of Jesus' birth to the shepherds was extraordinary news to ordinary people. The glory of God came down to the shepherds in the fields and they were afraid. It's easy to see why they were scared. Can you imagine how overwhelming this whole experience must have been for the shepherds?

Pray Together

God we thank You for the gift of salvation through Jesus. We are grateful that we can be born again and be clothed in Your righteousness.

Cook Together

Mom's Banana Bread

....

Cream until fluffy: ½ cup shortening and 1 ½ cup sugar

Beat thoroughly: 2 large eggs

Sift together: 2 ½ cups flour, ¼ tsp. baking powder, ¾ tsp. baking soda, and 1 tsp. salt

Stir in with ¼ cup buttermilk

3 bananas

½ cup nuts, if desired

Bake at 350 degrees for about 35 to 40 minutes

Fun Together

Make gifts for those in need.

Spend some time together making some baked goods for people who are alone, like the elderly or those in nursing homes. While baking, make home-made cards. Take them to the elderly in your neighborhood and to the local nursing home. This is a true example of how it is always better to give than to receive.

DECEMBER 13

"But the angel said to them, "Do not be afraid. I bring you good tidings of great joy that will be for all the people."
Luke 2:10

Sing Together

The First Noel

....

The story in Luke chapter 2 not only tells good news but the best news that the world would ever hear. The Savior had been born and the first to hear of this life changing news were the poorest and most vulnerable people in society. This is evidence that no matter how gloomy our life may seem, God has not forsaken us.

Pray Together

God we are thankful to spend time with our families learning about Your birth and the reason You came. Thank You for our families and we ask that You bless us each one.

Cook Together

Aunt Darlene's Home-Made Chocolate Pie

....

1 can cream

1 can milk

2 Tablespoons cornstarch

½ cup sugar

1 large package Chocolate
(Cook/Serve) pie filling

2 Tablespoons Cocoa

4 egg yolks

Add one stick butter as it starts to thicken

Pour into two pie shells.

Meringue
....

Beat 3 or 4 egg whites with ¼ tsp. cream of tartar until foamy. Egg whites should be room temperature and mix them in a glass or metal bowl. Slowly add ¾ cup white sugar until stiff peaks form. Spoon onto pies and bake at 350 degrees for about 10 minutes.

Fun Together

Play favorite family games.

Invite a family in your neighborhood to come play games. Eat snacks, tell stories, laugh and just enjoy one another's company. Love your neighbor!

ON MISSION

TOGETHER

"Then the eleven disciples went to Galilee, to the mountain where Jesus had told them to go. When they saw him, they worshiped him; but some doubted. Then Jesus came to them and said, "All authority in heaven and on earth has been given to me. Therefore go and make disciples of all nations, baptizing them in the name of the Father and of the Son and of the Holy Spirit, and teaching them to obey everything I have commanded you. And surely I am with you always, to the very end of the age."

Matthew 28:16-20

A Global Gift Exchange

We have all participated in a white elephant gift exchange at a party before right? This is a twist on that fun game. The idea here is to do a gift exchange with a missions focus. Tell people to bring gifts that represent a region of the world or a people group. For example, if you want to represent South Asia, your gift could be a souvenir from your trip to India, a mini Taj Mahal, or a five-dollar gift certificate to an Indian restaurant. Inside each gift, write a prayer request for the country, region or people group that inspired your gift. After you are done exchanging gifts, pray through all the prayer requests.

DECEMBER 14

"Today in the town of David a Savior has been born to you; he is Christ the Lord."
Luke 2:11

Sing Together

Angels We Have Heard on High

. . . .

Every detail of Christ's birth, from the long journey to Bethlehem, to no room in the inn, was part of God's plan. Even the parts of the story that seemed negative were all orchestrated by God and fit perfectly into His plan of salvation. So much of it seemed to not make sense at the time that it was happening.

When in our own lives, it seems that things are confusing or out of control, we can trust that God is in control. God is always good and His ways are always best.

Pray Together

Lord, we can only imagine how special and awe-inspiring it must have been for the shepherds to come and see the King of Kings lying in a manger. We worship You for Your humble birth and praise You for Your glorious reign.

Cook Together

Peanut Butter Fudge

....

3 cups sugar   1 2/3 cup creamy peanut butter
½ cup butter   1 (7 oz.) marshmallow cream
2/3 cup evaporated milk   1 tsp. vanilla extract

Mix together the butter, milk and sugar in a saucepan. Constantly stir on medium heat until it boils. Turn down the heat and simmer for about 5 minutes, always stirring. Next, add in peanut butter and stir making sure to blend it very well. Then, add vanilla and marshmallow cream. Mix altogether until blended well and spread into a 13X9 pan. Let it cool and then cut into squares.

Fun Together

Go on a drive to look for Christmas lights.

While driving around to admire the beautiful lights, talk about how Jesus told us that we are to be a light unto the world, a city on a hill. Our lives are on display for all to see and we should always try to shine with the love of Jesus all year long!

DECEMBER 15

"This will be a sign to you: You will find a baby wrapped
in cloths and lying in a manger."
Luke 2:12

Sing Together

Go Tell It On the Mountain

Many parents still swaddle their newborn babies to make them feel comfortable, safe, and cozy. Maybe Mary wrapped Jesus in swaddling clothes because she was a very attentive, caring mother. The Son of God came into the world, just like any other baby who has ever been born. He was vulnerable, needy, and dependent upon His mother for care. This is a sign that Jesus was fully human, yet fully God, and can identify with our trials. What an amazing thought!

Pray Together

Lord, help us to tell the "Good News" of Jesus to all people. Give us the desire and the joy to shout Your name from the mountaintops.

Cook Together

Mrs. Barb's Cheeseball

....

*3 packages of cream cheese (softened)   2 teaspoons Accent

3 packages of wafer beef (chopped)   Onion flakes to taste

Worcestershire Sauce to taste

Form into a ball and chill in the refrigerator. Serve with crackers.

Fun Together

Put on your own Christmas play.

Use robes or sheets for costumes, a doll for baby Jesus, and any other props that you can think of. Invite relatives over to see the play and don't forget to record it!

DECEMBER 16

"Glory to God in the highest and on earth peace to men on whom his favor rests."
Luke 2:14

Sing Together

Tell Me the Story of Jesus

. . . .

The song of the angels, "Glory to God in the highest," was heard on the fields outside of Bethlehem by the shepherds. But it will one day be heard all over the world in collaboration with all of heaven. How wonderful to know that when we sing praises to our King, we are joining with the hosts of heaven throughout all eternity. Lift high Jesus' name!

Pray Together

How grateful we are for the wonderful story of You, Jesus. May we always treasure that story in our hearts and minds. Compel us to tell it wherever we go.

Cook Together

Chocolate Divine

....

1 package crushed graham crackers	8 oz. cream cheese
¼ cup powdered sugar	1 cup cool whip
1 stick melted butter	Pour on crust and refrigerate until set.
Mix together and pat firmly in pan	Mix:
Beat:	3 cups cold milk
1 cup powdered sugar	2 packages instant chocolate pudding

Spread on top of cream cheese mixture and refrigerate.
When set, top with more cool whip.

Fun Together

Make outdoor lanterns.

This is a great way to decorate your sidewalk for Christmas.
You will need:

*Brown or white paper lunch bag	*Sand
*Hole punch in shape of snowflake or star	*Votive candles

Punch many shapes into the sides of the lunch bag. Fill the bottom with sand and set the votive in the sand securely. Light the candle and enjoy!

DECEMBER 17

"So they hurried off and found Mary and Joseph, and
the baby who was lying in the manger."
Luke 2:16

Sing Together

It Came Upon a Midnight Clear

The shepherds hurried. When the angels had told them about Jesus' birth, they didn't wait to discuss the news. They hurried to see what had happened.

How often do we hurry, to see what God is doing or rush to do what God is calling us to do? Let us learn from the shepherds to trust in our faith in Christ, and move swiftly when he calls.

Pray Together

Jesus, we long for the day when peace shall overcome the earth and You return for Your children. What a sweet song in heaven there will be as we join the eternal chorus in singing Your praises.

Cook Together

Grandma's Coconut Cream Pie

....

1 large box vanilla pudding	1 can milk
½ cup sugar	4 egg yolks
2 Tablespoons cornstarch	1 stick butter as it starts to thicken
1 tsp. vanilla	Add coconut as it thickens and pour into pie shells.
1 can cream	

Meringue

....

Beat 3 or 4 egg whites with ¼ tsp. cream of tartar until foamy. Egg whites should be room temperature and mix them in a glass or metal bowl. Slowly add ¾ cup white sugar until stiff peaks form. Spoon onto pies and bake at 350 degrees for about 10 minutes.

Fun Together

Build gum drop towers.

Use toothpicks and spice drops to build towers. Set a timer and see who can build the tallest tower.

DECEMBER 18

"Come let us bow down in worship, let us kneel before the Lord our maker; for he is our God and we are the people of his pasture, the flock under his care.
Psalm 95:6-7

Sing Together

God Rest Ye Merry Gentlemen

....

When we see pictures of the nativity or a ceramic nativity scene, we often see the shepherds shown as kneeling and looking at baby Jesus in the manger. The Hebrew word for "worship" literally means to fall prostrate on oneself. As God's people, we need to make sure that we understand that we are to bow humbly, admit our sin before God, and declare our dependence upon Him.

Pray Together

We are thankful today Lord, that we have nothing to fear. You have come to bring us good tidings of salvation. We know that we have eternal hope in You and that gives us peace.

Cook Together

Pumpkin Cream Cheese Coconut Pecan Cake

2 cups sugar

1 tsp. baking powder

1 ¼ cups salad oil

2 cups flour

4 eggs, beaten

1 tsp. cinnamon

2 cups cooked pumpkin

1/3 cup chopped nuts

1 tsp. salt

1/3 cup flaked coconut

1 tsp. baking soda

Beat together sugar and oil. Mix in eggs and pumpkin. Stir in dry ingredients. Then add nuts and coconut. Pour into greased 9 X 13 pan and bake at 350 degrees for 25 to 30 minutes or until cake tests done. Frost with cream cheese icing.

Coconut Cream Cheese Frosting

½ stick butter, softened

1 tsp. vanilla

1- 8 oz. package cream cheese

½ cup chopped nuts

1 box powdered sugar

1/4 cup flaked coconut

Cream butter and cheese. Gradually add in powdered sugar and vanilla. Stir in nuts and coconut. Spread evenly over cake when cooled.

Fun Together

Build your own ice cream sundae.

Use a variety of ice cream flavors and toppings. Be extravagant and have fun! Remember as you are building an amazing sundae that God didn't spare any details when He created you. He loved you and formed you perfectly to every last detail!

DECEMBER 19

"After Jesus was born in Bethlehem in Judea, during the time of
King Herod, Magi came from the east to Jerusalem"
Matthew 2:1

Sing Together

We Three Kings of Orient Are

Our God is a God who does unexpected things. Who would have ever thought that God would have used a star to guide the wise men to Jesus? And who would have thought that men from the East would have come to worship a young Jewish King? God moves in unexpected ways today and can often take us by surprise. So thankful that He sent the Savior of the world as our greatest surprise!

Pray Together

Dear Jesus, we see the gifts that the Magi brought and how they pointed to Your death. We praise You for your resurrection from the grave. Thank You, Jesus, for Your sacrifice.

Cook Together

Classic Sour Cream Cheesecake

Prep time: 25 minutes

Total time: 3 hours

Makes one 9-inch cheesecake

1 ½ ups shortbread cookie crumbs
(or graham crackers)

2 tablespoons butter, melted

3 (8 ounce) packages of cream cheese, softened

1 (14 ounce) can sweetened condensed milk

4 eggs

1 teaspoon vanilla

1(8 ounce) container sour cream

1 (8 ounce) can cherry pie filling, chilled

Preheat oven to 350 degrees. Combine crumbs and butter; press firmly on bottom of 9-inch springform pan. In large mixer bowl, beat cream cheese until fluffy. Gradually beat in sweetened condensed milk until smooth. Beat in eggs then sour cream and vanilla. Pour into prepared pan. Bake 50 to 55 minutes or until lightly browned around the edge (center will be lightly soft). Cool. Chill. Top with cherry filling or garnish as desired and refrigerate.

Fun Together

Make Home-made wrapping paper.

Use plain brown grocery bags. Place the bag unfolded on a table covered with newspaper.

Pour a small amount of paint onto a paper plate. Dip your sponge in paint and decorate. Use sponges that are shaped into stars or hearts. Let dry completely before using.

DECEMBER 20

"and asked, "Where is the one who has been born king of the Jews?
We saw his star in the east and have come to worship him."
Matthew 2:2

Sing Together

Beautiful Star of Bethlehem

....

These wise men, perhaps from Persia, traveled thousands of miles seeking a King. It was a long, expensive, and difficult journey. But their desire to find the Savior of the world was so strong that the danger of the trip was worth it all.

What can we learn from the wise men? Are we seeking to know Jesus more? Are we willing to make sacrifices for Jesus? Just how far are we willing to go, to make His name known to the world?

Pray Together

Jesus, we know that You are the star of Bethlehem. We invite You to be the star and the center of our lives. Help us to always let Your light guide our ways.

Cook Together

Star Sugar Cookies with Butter Cream Icing

· ·

2 cups all-purpose flour

1 cup granulated sugar

½ tsp. baking powder

1 large egg

¼ teaspoon salt

1 teaspoon vanilla extract

½ cup (1 stick) unsalted butter melted

In a bowl, whisk together the flour, baking powder, and salt. In a another bowl, using an electric mixer, beat the butter and granulated sugar on medium speed until well blended. Add the egg and vanilla and beat on medium speed until combined. Add half the flour mixture and mix on low speed until blended. Add the rest of the flour mixture and mix just until blended. Scrape down the bowl. Dump the dough onto a work surface and press it together into a mound. Divide the dough in half and refrigerate until firm. Preheat the oven to 350 degrees. Line 2 cookie sheets with parchment paper. Sprinkle a clean work surface with flour. Place the chilled dough on the floured surface. Sprinkle the top of the dough with a little more flour. Roll out the dough with a rolling pin until it is about ¼ inch think. Use a star cookie cutter to cut out as many stars as you can, then use a metal spatula to transfer them to a cookie sheet. Bake for 10 to 12 minutes. Let them cool for 5 minutes and then move them with a metal spatula.

Buttercream icing

· ·

1 stick butter (softened)

½ cup Crisco

1 tsp. vanilla

4 cups powdered sugar (add one cup at a time)

3 Tbs. milk

Fun Together

Go outside and star gaze tonight.

Bundle up and trek outside together to take in the cosmos. While stargazing, talk about how God created the entire universe and everything in it. That same God came to Earth, took on human flesh and paid a debt we could never pay. Stand in awe as you look into the heavens knowing that the indescribable God who created all of that, loved you enough to come for you.

ON MISSION

TOGETHER

"Give thanks to the LORD, call on His name; make known
among the nations what he has done.
Psalm 96:10

Feed the Pig

Not all of us can go on mission trips every time there is an opportunity. And sometimes because of various reasons, we just can't go at all, ever. But there is a way to be a part of spreading the Gospel and God's love to people all over the world through others who can go. We can save our change and donate it to missionaries.

One way that this can be done is to "Feed the Pig". In January, buy a piggy bank that can be painted. As a family, paint the piggy bank and decorate it. Add extra change to it all year long. In December, break the piggy bank open and donate the money to a mission team or mission minded cause.

My Mom and Dad offered this great piece of advice to me when growing up: "A penny saved is a penny earned." They were right, of course. It takes hard work for sure, but saving your change makes sense. There are always opportunities to save coins from keeping the change from your purchases to reaching deep inside your pockets. Saving your change can happen every day, even if it's just a little bit.

Here are some useful tips as a family to help you save more for missions:

1. **Always be saving** even amidst your other bills.
2. **Save one opportunity at a time** to prevent putting a strain on your budget.
3. **Create new ways to save** by using your imagination!
4. **Don't get discouraged** even when there are detours along the way. Keep on trucking along.

DECEMBER 21

"On coming to the house, they saw the child with his mother
Mary, and they bowed down and worshiped him.
Matthew 2:11a

Sing Together

O Holy Night

....

King Herod tried to kill Jesus, while the wise men used their knowledge to seek Him, find Him and worship Him. How do we use our knowledge of Jesus? We should always begin with worship. Bowing our hearts to the King of Heaven and glorifying Him for who He is must be a daily habit for us as a people. Knowing that He is Emmanuel, God with us, changes our perspective about who we are. What a comforting thought to know that the Creator of the Universe, knows us intimately!

Pray Together

Thank You Lord for giving us an example of how to love. For we know that we can love others because You first loved us. We pray that we will always show that compassion toward our neighbors.

Cook Together

Holiday Pineapple Lemonade

....

1 cup lemonade mix

2 cups cold water

1 can of chilled pineapple juice (46 oz.)

2 cans chilled lemon-lime soda

Mix together and enjoy!

Fun Together

Write love notes to your family members.

Decorate them and tell them why you love them!

DECEMBER 22

"Then they opened their treasures and presented him
with gifts of gold, incense, and myrrh.
Matthew 2:11b

Sing Together

Silent Night

....

The wise men show us in their coming that Jesus is to be worshiped by all the nations of the world, not just Jews. At the end of the book of Matthew the words of Jesus are, "All authority has been given to me in heaven and on earth. Go therefore and make disciples of all nations." There are Biblical prophesies that said that all peoples of the world would worship Him as king. The worship of the wise men is proof that Jesus was the promised Messiah, the King and Fulfiller of prophesy.

Pray Together

We are praising You God that Christ was born to save!
Thank You for this amazing gift of love!

Mama's Home-made Meatballs

2 eggs

2 cups quick-cooking oats

1 can (12 oz.) evaporated milk

¾ cup chopped onion

1 ½ tsp. salt

½ tsp. pepper

½ tsp. garlic powder

3 pounds hamburger meat

Sauce:

2 cups ketchup

1 ½ cups packed brown sugar

½ cup chopped onion

1 ½ tsp. Liquid Smoke, optional

½ tsp. garlic powder

In a bowl, beat eggs. Add oats, milk, onion, salt, pepper and garlic powder. Crumble beef over mixture and mix well. Shape into 1-1/2 inch balls. Place in two 13 X 9 inch baking pans. Bake, uncovered, at 375 degrees for 30 minutes or until juices run clear. Remove from the oven and drain. Place all of the meatballs in one of the pans.

In a saucepan, bring all sauce ingredients to a boil. Pour over meatballs. Return to the oven and bake, uncovered, for 20 minutes.

Fun Together

Go Christmas caroling.

Gather your family and friends and carol around your neighborhood. You can even go to a nursing home or retirement community to sing carols. There are people who will not go to church but they will open their doors to hear the sounds of carolers. What a glorious way to share the Gospel of Jesus!

DECEMBER 23

"For God so loved the world that he gave his one and only Son, that whoever believes in him shall not perish but have eternal life."
John 3:16

Sing Together

Good Christian Men Rejoice

....

Christ was born to save! That is the message of Christmas. We worship a God who became flesh and loved us enough to leave heaven and take on flesh. He can identify with us in every way. He knows our fears, our struggles, and our pain.

Yet he came to suffer a cruel death on a cross to rescue us. His blood paid a debt that we could never pay. Glory to God for his immeasurable love!

Pray Together

Jesus, how wonderful a thought that You were born to save us! We give You all the glory for Your mighty victory over death and the grave. You were born to save!

Cook Together

Butter Cream Cross Cake

....

Bake any brand of cake and in any flavor of your choosing in a 13 x 9 pan. Cut the cake and piece together in the shape of a cross. Decorate with Butter Cream icing when cool.

Butter Cream Icing

1 stick butter

½ cup Crisco

1 tsp. vanilla

4 cups powdered sugar (add one cup at a time)

3 tbs. milk

Mix all ingredients together until fluffy.

Fun Together

Play Christmas Pictionary.

Divide up in teams. Use words that tell the story of Jesus' birth, life, death and resurrection from the grave.

DECEMBER 24

"Thanks be to God for his indescribable gift!
2 Corinthians 9:15

Sing Together

Joy to the World

....

Giving gifts and receiving gifts is a wonderful thing to do. It's really nice when the person giving you the gift knows you really well. They might know in advance what you need and what you would like. God knows just what we need. We need a Savior. The greatest gift God has given is eternal life that has been bought by his son Jesus. Have you un-wrapped this amazing gift?

Pray Together

What joy there is in knowing that You reign over all creation and over every part of our lives. Dear Lord, please help us to rest in Your truth and love. Give us peace during this Christmas season and open our eyes to see Your glory.

Cook Together

Chinese Egg Rolls

....

2lbs. ground beef

4 shredded carrots

2 tbsp. garlic salt

½ head shredded cabbage

2 medium diced onions

Salt/pepper

½ cup soy sauce

wonton wraps

Mix all ingredients raw and set aside. Place 1 tsp. of above mixture in wrap. Then place flour and water paste on 2 sides of each wrap. Close the wrap diagonally and press sides together. Deep fry and enjoy! (They will come to top of oil when done.)

Fun Together

Sing Christmas hymns together and read the Christmas story from Luke Ch. 2.

DECEMBER 25

"For to us a child is born, to us a son is given, and the government will be on his shoulders. And He will be called Wonderful Counselor, Mighty God, Everlasting Father, Prince of Peace.
Isaiah 9:6

Sing Together

I Stand Amazed in the Presence

One of Jesus' many titles is Prince of Peace. Our world is full of conflict, but Jesus tells us in the New Testament many ways that He will bring us peace. In John 14:27, He said, "Peace I leave with you; my peace I give to you. Let not your hearts be troubled; neither let them be afraid." Jesus promises a peace that only He can bring, not one that the world will understand. When we have Jesus as our Savior, we can have the peace that He brings. He took our sins and iniquities upon the cross and we are forgiven. He bridged the divide between us and God when He paid our sin debt. Jesus is our true and lasting peace.

Pray Together

Oh Lord, You are wonderful! Thank You for giving us Jesus to stand in our place and to save us from our sins. We give You our lives and long to honor You in all we do and say. Help us to remember the reason that Jesus came to earth this day and every day.

Cook Together

Christmas Breakfast Casserole

....

1 pound sausage fried

6 eggs whipped

1 cup milk

2 cups bread crumbs

1 cup shredded cheddar cheese

Mix altogether and pour into casserole dish. Bake at 350 degrees for 35 minutes.

Fun Together

Open gifts with family and remember the reason why we give gifts in the first place. Jesus is the true gift and we love because He first loved us!

Why TOGETHER?

It is true, we certainly love our families. And often times, that love tends to be measured in material things such as toys, the latest technology, and trendy clothes. We can get so caught up in these "things" we forget that the time we give our kids is more important than anything else. This doesn't just apply to our younger kids, but older kids too. Spending time with our children is a gift and God has commanded us in His word that it is important for parents to teach their children about Him. Here are some verses to remind us that God's heart is for family to spend time TOGETHER growing in grace and serving Him.

Ephesians 6:4
"Fathers, do not provoke your children to anger; instead, bring them up in the discipline and instruction of the Lord."

Deuteronomy 11:18-19
"You shall therefore impress these words of mine on your heart and on your soul; and you shall bind them as a sign on your hand, and they shall be as frontals on your forehead. You shall teach them to your sons, talking of them when you sit in your house and when you walk along the road and when you lie down and when you rise up."

Proverbs 22:6
"Train up a child in the way he should go, and when he is old he will not depart from it."

Printed in the United States
By Bookmasters